The Great Reversal

A Journey with Christ and De Chirico

Kerry M. Pierce

The Great Reversal

A Journey with Christ and De Chirico

Kerry M. Pierce

All images Copyright Kerry M. Pierce unless noted otherwise

www.KerryPierce.com

www.ChristianMandalas.com†

Copyright © 2018 Kerry M. Pierce

†Christian Mandalas is a trademark of Kerry M. Pierce

ISBN-13: 978-0-9972809-5-1

For Gail, Nancy, and Kirsten
Mother, Wife, and Daughter

Contents

Acknowledgments

Special thanks to my wife Nancy and my daughter Kirsten for their support.

Preface

Much of my life has been spent working with a community of engineers. Engineers are naturally curious. They are problem solvers. They are analytical and seek to understand. In the quest to solve problems, they ask questions. A common question is: How does it work? They want things to make sense. For engineers, there is joy in understanding how something works. The very process of figuring out how things work brings them satisfaction. Underlying an engineer's desire to know how things work, there is often a desire to apply new learning to a product that will benefit society.

For part of my life, I have also been fortunate to work with a community of artists. Like engineers, they are naturally curious. As they continually explore, they too ask questions. A common characteristic of the artists I worked with was, they had strong personal value systems. As they gather information, they look for underlying meaning, which they test against their value systems. Rather than, how does this work, an artist will ask: What does it mean? Why did someone build this? What impact will it have on my life and culture?

Let us take autonomous cars as an example. An engineer would be fascinated with a vehicle that could sense the environment and navigate without real-time human input. How is the environmental data collected, radar, lidar, GPS, cameras? How is the vehicle's motion predicted? Is image recognition being used? How is the vehicle's final trajectory being planned?

An artist would be just as fascinated, but they would likely approach a self-driving car with a different set of questions. What do autonomous vehicles mean for my life? What effect will autonomous vehicles have on our culture? Are people giving up control over machines?

When I first heard about the Rapture as a young boy, I wondered. If I was driving a car at the time of the Rapture, and I suddenly departed the planet, what harm would my vehicle cause to other drivers who remained on the roadway? I still do not know when the Rapture will occur, but I have an answer to how my car might behave without my presence.

In the Gospel of Luke and the book of Acts, we find a recurrent theme that theologians refer to as the great reversal. These great reversals are unexpected, almost shocking statements from Jesus and interactions with Jesus that cause us to stop and re-think our value systems. Sayings like: "Love your enemies," "For whoever would save his life will lose it, but whoever loses his life for my sake will save it," "And behold, some are last who will be first, and some are first who will be last," "It is more blessed to give than to receive," and "For everyone who exalts himself will be humbled, but the one who humbles himself will be exalted."

We will explore Jesus' great reversal sayings. On our journey, we will use both an engineer's approach and an artist's approach. We will ask questions. We will explore with great curiosity.

On the engineering side, we will break down scripture and art into smaller, understandable pieces to make sense of it. On the artist side, we will try to understand the meaning of Jesus' words for our lives. The breath of extraordinary artwork used will deepen the study.

As disciples of Christ, we want to integrate Jesus' great reversal sayings, and interactions, into our lives. By engaging in this exploration, we grow as disciples. We grow spiritually. We lay up treasures in heaven, and we gain an eternal perspective.

While these benefits are impressive, almost incredible, they also feel imperceptible because these blessings seem to exist beyond our physical senses. But, on our journey, we bear good fruit. Discernable, perceptible, Christian fruit. Our actions, our words, and our children will generate additional fruit well beyond our earthly lifespan.

Consider the Penitent Thief on the cross next to Jesus. He may have only spent six hours with Jesus during his earthly life, but his moment of faith and his interaction with Christ has given hope to others for nearly 2000 years. Two thousand years during which the Penitent Thief has continued to remain in the presence of our Lord.

We bear good fruit for the Kingdom. The Kingdom, which the Father has given us.

Overall, this book reflects on roughly ten of Jesus' great reversal sayings found in Luke-Acts. The book is a series of meditations on the words of our Lord. These meditations are accompanied by art that will add depth to the moment. There is a flow to the studies, which are all connected by the great reversal theme.

The reflections may be read independently or used in conjunction with *Christian Mandalas: The Great Reversal Study*.[1]

English Standard Version

The Great Reversal – Discovering El Dorado

Mom, Dad, what were you thinking? I needed to finish the assembly and get moving before they realized their mistake.

For my 12th birthday, I was given an old-school, mechanical, dual odometer + speedometer for my bicycle. Best birthday present ever.

The analog readout was already mounted on the handlebars of my Schwinn 5 speed. I finished connecting the cable that ran from the readout down the front fork to the bayonet mounted on the hub of the front tire. The bayonet extended inside the spokes of the front wheel. As the wheel turned, the mechanism spun with it, turning the cable that ran up to the speedometer. Speed, show me some speed.

I jumped onto my bike and pedaled off, wondering how my parents could give me such a thoughtful gift without realizing what I would do with it.

Heading north on Oak Street gave a continuous downhill run. On the steeper city blocks, I could hit around 20 MPH before having to brake at the next intersection. I needed to register 25 MPH, but the short blocks running north and south in Port Angeles, Washington, didn't provide enough distance to build up speed.

Between 7th and 6th Street, it dawned on me that the blocks were much longer on the streets running east and west. A quick right turn onto 6th, and sure enough, the speedometer was reading over 20 MPH and headed to 25.

The needle was hovering around 24 MPH. I decided to continue pedaling through the intersection of 6th and Laurel. What could go wrong?

One long block remained of east 6th Street before I would come to South Lincoln and need to stop for cars. The needle was now hovering just below 25 MPH, and I'm running out of road—high drama. Fortunately, there is a driveway off of 6th street, just before Lincoln, that went into the parking lot behind

the old McGlenn's Thriftway. I planned to give one last push, make a wide left turn into the parking lot, and hit 25 MPH.

I was 12 years old. My judgment at this time was still questionable.

With the turn lined up, I focused all my attention on the speedometer needle. I was going to make it. In the blink of an eye, I was standing to the left of my bike at the driveway entrance. Two feet in front of me was a late 1960's Cadillac Eldorado. Inside the vehicle was an old couple. Agape, eyes-wide-open, they were in shock. I don't remember seeing or hearing them before I turned in, but I wasn't watching the road.

I was riding at almost 25 MPH, looking down at my speedometer, and then a fraction of a second later, the next image to enter my eyes was the 4700 lb yellow Cadillac. What felt like an enormous pair of hands had grabbed my torso, pulled me up and back, and then set me down. Set me down safely before my 80 lb body splattered across the Eldorado's windshield. A great reversal.

With a goofy grin on my face, I walked away with my bike for a few feet. The bike and rider were unscathed. After a few minutes, I walked back to the driveway. No residual black rubber from my bicycle tire appeared on the dry pavement. I hadn't braked. The absence of a skid mark made sense to me.

I had just experienced a perceptible interruption of the laws of nature. I knew that bikes don't usually go from 25 to 0 MPH in the blink of an eye. There was no skid mark. My bike was undamaged, and I had given an old couple something to talk about over dinner that evening. I still remember the images and the feeling.

The Second Miracle

It was a day of miracles and grace.

I had some idea of what had happened to me, but it was a new experience, and I wanted to discuss it with someone.

I was raised by an excellent Lutheran Minister and his wife. The folks who gave me the speedometer in the first place.

People knew Gail as a loving, relentlessly faithful Norwegian pastor's wife and humble servant of God. She was. However, to a 12-year-old boy who had done something wrong, she was the Old Testament wrath of God incarnate. I exaggerate. Slightly.

Gail was amazing. She fulfilled the duties of a Pastor's wife and raised six challenging boys. She was shaping our young lives—any discipline we received, we deserved.

I loved her, and I wanted to share my experience with her. However, the confession of a near bicycle accident due to my negligence needed to be calculated. Sharing the story could lead to one or all of the following: Sermonette on the responsibility of riding a bike, loss of bicycle privileges for one week, removal of the speedometer, room time, and possibly, a hot chocolate conversation with dad. Hot chocolate meant you had crossed over into more serious territory.

Due to old-school Norwegian tradition, most of the dirty dishes didn't go into the dishwasher. They had to be hand-washed after dinner. It was my turn to dry the day of the miracle. Mom (Gail) washed, and I dried. I told her my story.

Mom: "Well Kerry, it sounds like you had an experience with the Holy Spirit."

Kerry is thinking: What? That's it? It's coming. I know it's coming.

Mom: "Kerry, don't rub the cast iron frying pan with the dishtowel. Just pat it dry."

Kerry thinking: Unbelievable. One day, two miracles. Don't push things any further.

In the back of my mind, I briefly entertained the thought of using stories of divine intervention to escape punishment for future wrong-doings. I never did.

Hebrews 11:1

Now faith is the

assurance of things

hoped for, the conviction

of things not seen.

What, How, and Why?

I was a curious and somewhat reckless boy. How were things made? Why do things work the way they do? It is not a surprise that my first degree was in Engineering-Physics. When I studied the law of conservation of momentum, I applied the equation to the bike versus Cadillac scenario. Cadillac wins, bike and rider lose.

The great reversal miracle left me hungry. I knew the observable facts. I knew the laws of physics were interrupted. I knew the miracle had come from God.

But the experience was completely foreign. To understand the event, I needed to re-think my mental model of reality. As I reflected and thought about my great reversal, three ideas came to mind.

1. A Spiritual Realm beyond the Senses

What I had experienced went beyond my senses. I did not see, smell, hear or taste anything associated with the two enormous hands that rescued me. What I physically felt was limited to pressure. There was no sensation of heat or cold.

A discernable second realm, beyond my physical senses, existed. Within that realm, there existed intelligence, an awareness of my situation, and the desire to prevent harm from coming to me.

I had avoided a physical impact, but the spiritual impact was significant. God used the great reversal experience to grow my faith, consider him, and spark a belief in the spiritual rather than just the sensory.

2. God's values versus the World's values

My initial reaction, at 12 years old, was that God had just saved my life. I realized that, in God's opinion, my life had value. Not everyone I had encountered in the world up to this point shared this view. God's thoughts and God's standards were different than those of the culture in which I grew up.

The impact was for me to consider putting my reliance in God rather than the world. Additionally, there was a new desire to understand God's values.

3. Focus on the Kingdom

God's creative action meant that I had a future beyond my 12th birthday, some purpose, some meaningful role to play in God's kingdom.

Over time, with study, I realized there was even more going on in my life. I knew that Jesus performed miracles. God also performed miracles through agents. Moses is a good example. God also uses angels. Hebrews 1:14 (ESV) states, "Are they [angels] not all ministering spirits sent out [by God] to serve for the sake of those who are to inherit salvation?"

This single verse summed up my overall experience. God had sent an angel (apparently angels can have large hands) to perform the great reversal miracle. Not only did I have a future role in God's kingdom during my time in this world, but I also had a significant future beyond this world.

The best commentary I have read on *The Letter to the Hebrews* is by William L. Lane. His commentary on Hebrews 1:14 reads: "The implications of this fact [verse] are startling....God takes thought for his people in their situation. Angels have been sent forth by God....The statement in verse 14 thus reminds us of God's constant thoughtfulness. The formulation 'to those who are to inherit salvation' clearly implies the activity of angels in our lives even prior to the experience of faith."[2]

In my case, this verse was prophetic. I do not believe I was regenerate at age 12. I am regenerate, that is, born-again now and have inherited salvation.

The residual spiritual impact of the great reversal miracle was that I took a longer view and focused more and more on the kingdom of heaven.

Angels
Kerry Pierce

Giorgio de Chirico

Entering Munchkinland
Metro-Goldwyn-Mayer

From late 1909 to early 1919, the artist Giorgio de Chirico painted through his metaphysical period. This decade is a unique moment in art when an individual bursts forth with a new painting style. De Chirico was exploring metaphysics, an abstruse branch of philosophy, from an artist's perspective. Thought was translated to canvas that the world had not yet seen. De Chirico's works from this period form one of the most curious and fascinating moments in art history.

De Chirico's works from the metaphysical period are meaningful because they deal with two different realms, like Jesus' great reversal sayings. The images encourage us to focus beyond the sensory and move to the spiritual. Time is annulled, causing us to focus on eternity. As such, they provide a visual means of understanding the intent of Jesus' great reversal sayings.

Put another way, de Chirico's art likely provides the best possible illustrations for Jesus' great reversal sayings found in the Gospel of Luke and the book of Acts.

As adults, we have built a mental library. We gain knowledge and learn by processing our senses. If a painter assigns attributes, or properties, to an element that does not usually possess those properties, we can no longer rely on the information stored in our mental libraries. The lack of context causes disorientation but can also awaken a deep childlike desire to explore. A similar effect can be achieved by removing an element from its traditional setting and placing it into an unexpected environment. The feeling is a bit like the moment in the *Wizard of Oz* when Dorothy opens the door of her sepia-toned farmhouse to see the Technicolor Land of Oz. With this in mind, we enter the Museum of Modern Art in New York. You move from room to room and arrive at a de Chirico exhibit.

The first piece you stand in front of is *The Melancholy of Departure*, painted by Giorgio de Chirico in 1914. The image feels flat. Compared to artwork from the Renaissance, the technique feels almost childish. But, every nuance of this work is intentional. So, we continue to explore the work.

On the initial read of the image, we see a bright yellow/gold element running vertically on the right side of the picture. At the bottom of the image, a second bright, similarly colored component runs horizontally. These two elements form a somewhat childlike arrow that points to a bunch of bananas.

Yes, I am with you. This is a rather pathetic banana still life. We either walk away and ask the curator how bad art gets into good museums, or we press on with childlike curiosity.

Ignore the bananas. Start asking questions.

The Melancholy of Departure
Giorgio de Chirico

The remainder of the composition doesn't provide any relief.

In an image depicting architectural elements, it is common for the lines associated with the buildings to converge at a single point known as a vanishing point. De Chirico's composition has multiple vanishing points created by the architectural elements. OK, but my eye wants the architecture in the painting to make sense in three-dimensional space. It does not. The lines associated with the edges of the buildings in the image are too far off for my mind to resolve the structures into a consistent three-dimensional space. Without much effort, I found five different vanishing points in the painting identified by the red lines. The incoherent set of vanishing points disturbs me. De Chirico is violating my sense of perspective. De Chirico is also causing me to think.

The Melancholy of Departure (with vanishing points)

DC Comics' fictional *S.T.A.R. Labs* houses a particle accelerator. On the campus of Stanford University, the SLAC National Accelerator Laboratory linear accelerator is the longest linear particle accelerator in the world. The image shown is from inside the accelerator and gives a view of dozens of klystrons used to accelerate particles along their high-speed, two-mile journey. This picture captures a single vanishing point defined by the location where all the lines converge near the center of the image. This composition is easy to digest visually, like looking down an elevator shaft, through a tunnel, or along a straight section of a railroad track.

I built a 3D model of Chirico's *Melancholy of Departure* and rendered it. In my model, I have made all the buildings rectangular and laid them out on a grid, as one would expect in a city. The render shows a primary vanishing point towards the right of the image. The image feels resolved. It fits into my mental library of what a picture of a city should look like.

My act of resolving perspective in the image causes the composition to become uninteresting. The original stimulus which caused me to think and ask questions is gone.

Particle Accelerator with
Single Vanishing Point
Courtesy of
SLAC National Accelerator Laboratory

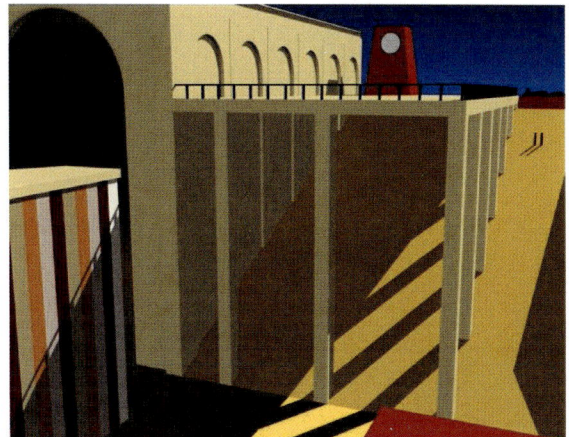

The Melancholy of Departure
3D Model

The Melancholy of Departure
3D Model with Vanishing Point

As we continue to explore *The Melancholy of Departure,* we find other anomalies.

Shadows fall in different directions. We are outside, and there should be one sun, but the shadows from the two people heading towards the train do not match the direction of the shadows coming from the other elements. The angle of the shadows from the two people don't quite match each other. It feels as if the two individuals are in slightly different time periods. One individual would be in the present; the other individual would be present in the same space, but at a different time when the sun has moved to a different location.

Additionally, the shadows are long, what you might expect around sunrise or sunset, but the clock says it's 1:27 PM. Time is annulled. The flags suggest a strong breeze blowing, but the puff of smoke from the train seems to linger, moving slightly in the opposite direction. Again, de Chirico is altering perspective, the behavior of light, and physics in a way I find disturbing.

With de Chirico's painting, we have entered into a foreign, irrational world. Even though the individual elements are familiar, the composition leaves us disoriented. De Chirico pushes us to go beyond what we see with our eyes and search for another meaning. The mental library we have built needs to open up and look at the image from an alternative perspective.

Like my great reversal bicycle experience, de Chirico's work interrupts my understanding of physical reality.

Further, like my great reversal bicycle experience, there are two realities, two realms in de Chirico's painting. The use of two domains is a frequent feature in de Chirico's works.

The first reality in *The Melancholy of Departure* is composed of the buildings, the walkways, the clock tower, and yes, the bananas. Let's call this reality the train station. The second reality, or realm, is the train with its little puff of smoke.

From the analogy of the bicycle incident, the two

tiny individuals on the walkway near the train represent the angel and the 12-year-old me. The angel, on the left, has just rescued me from harm and is about to leave the train station. Again, the train station represents our world. The train represents the second realm, heaven. There is a face embedded in a puff of white smoke rising from the train. The smoke is symbolic of God. Exodus 19:18, "Now Mount Sinai was wrapped in smoke because the Lord had descended on it in fire. The smoke of it went up like the smoke of a kiln, and the whole mountain trembled greatly." There are numerous associations between God and smoke in the Bible, especially in the Old Testament.

The puff of smoke from the train represents God watching over the angel's cross-realm activity.

The Melancholy of Departure is an appropriate title because I wanted the angel to remain and explain things to me. The spiritual being departed my realm too quickly. God wanted me to think through the incident for myself. Besides preventing harm from coming to me, the great reversal incident may have had much more to do with my faith. Perhaps supernatural intervention was required due to my weakness of faith.

A study of *The Melancholy of Departure* has at least two outcomes. First, it causes us to think and ask questions. The image forces us to go beyond what we see with our eyes and search for meaning. For a Christian, the significance comes from considering the painting from a spiritual point of view rather than a strictly visual perspective. Second, it causes us to think in terms of two realms or two kingdoms. Heaven and the world. Which of these kingdoms do we look to, which of these kingdoms will we store our treasures in, and which is trustworthy? Into which realm should we place our faith?

Angel
Kerry Pierce

The Great Reversal – Luke

In the Gospel of Luke, we find a recurrent theme that theologians refer to as the great reversal. These great reversals are unexpected, almost shocking statements from Jesus and interactions with Jesus that cause us to stop and re-think our value systems. Sayings like: "Love your enemies," "For whoever would save his life will lose it, but whoever loses his life for my sake will save it," "And behold, some are last who will be first, and some are first who will be last," "It is more blessed to give than to receive," and "For everyone who exalts himself will be humbled, but the one who humbles himself will be exalted."

These words are disorienting. They often push us into a foreign, unfamiliar place that makes us uncomfortable.

Perhaps the most stunning great reversal occurs when the Penitent Thief on the cross rises from the bottom of the first-century Palestinian ecosystem and expresses his faith in Christ. He repents, and without the benefit of the Lord's instruction which the apostles enjoyed, he reaches out in faith, requesting Jesus to remember him when Jesus enters into his reign. A criminal, hours away from death and in pain, suddenly has the presence of mind to confess his sin and his faith in Jesus. Spiritual whiplash.

These great reversal sayings challenge us. "Love your enemies." That is not easy. But, Christ calls us to active discipleship. He calls us to operate as salt and light in the world. Engaging in the great reversal teachings of Jesus enables us to become more Christ-like. Reflecting on these great reversal sayings is often humbling. But God reminds us that he honors the humble and that the humble will be exalted.

In the great reversal study, we find that the value system of the Kingdom is much different than that of our culture. The great reversal sayings challenge us to focus on the Kingdom, rather than the world, on the spiritual, rather than the sensory.

When reflected upon and applied to our lives, the great reversal sayings cause our focus to shift from

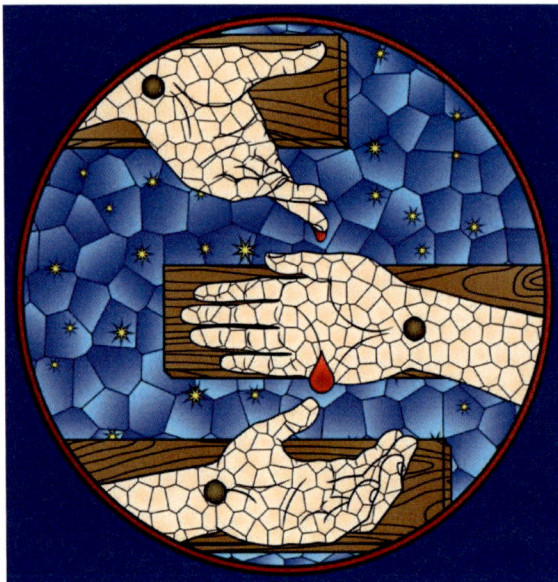

The Penitent Thief
Kerry Pierce

our needs to the needs of others and the needs of the Kingdom.

There is an assurance. An assurance of spiritual growth in this life, and reassurance that the Kingdom we are giving ourselves to, like our souls, is eternal and has eternal value.

Similar to how de Chirico's paintings are initially disorienting, causing us to re-think the compositions from a new perspective, Jesus' great reversal sayings cause us to re-think our values from the Kingdom's then a cultural perspective. In both cases, there is an invitation to seek. De Chirico's imagery and the words of Christ awaken a childlike desire to explore. As we move into Jesus' great reversal sayings, I will use de Chirico's art to illustrate Christ's words. Note that I generally attempt to retain as much of De Chirico's original intention with his art as I Christianize his work.

Consider de Chirico's painting, *The Enigma of the Arrival and the Afternoon*. A red wall separates two regions. The area behind the wall is mysterious. Our view is partially blocked. The wind fills the sail of a boat, and the flags on top of a temple flutter. The elements in this region are illuminated by a light source up and off to the right. Note also the cross structure of the sailboat's mast, as well as the subtle red stripes in the sail.

The Enigma of the Arrival and the Afternoon
Giorgio de Chirico

The second realm in the foreground shows an open space in a city. Shadows from an unseen structure fall onto the plaza creating a feeling of foreboding. One expects the front of the building on the far left of the painting to be illuminated by the same light source which lights up the temple, but the building remains in shadow. A curious shadow comes from the base of the same building on the left and moves diagonally across the checkerboard tile region to the front center of the image. This shadow suggests a second light source, behind and to the left of the building, inconsistent with the rest of the picture. If the light source that is illuminating the

14

temple were to cause the front of the building on the left to be in complete shadow, another structure is necessary. A building or element that we can't see. Even if such a structure existed, we would expect the shadow it casts to cut diagonally across the front of the building on the left, leaving some portion of its face lit up. Further, the two individuals in the image cast no observable shadow onto the ground of the plaza. Initially, we are confused.

For de Chirico, the two individuals are a philosopher and a poet, living out their lives in the second realm, playing out the game of life on a giant checkerboard, contemplating the realm beyond the wall. The area beyond the barrier represents the grand adventure of the mind and spirit. The great mysteries which we can only catch a partial glimpse of in this life due to the mental and spiritual walls with which we contend.

Christianizing the image, the two individuals become the same individual, separated by time and their belief in Christ.

The individual, at an earlier phase of life, dressed in red, moves onto the chessboard. He looks out across the chessboard contemplating how he wants to move through life. He believes he is in control. But the way forward will lead him into darkness.

The individual in blue is a Christian. He is separated from his prior self by time, but more importantly, he is distanced by his faith. He began his life as the man dressed in red and found himself in the darkness. Something of a Prodigal Son, he "came to himself" and moved off the chessboard. His head is bowed, he is humbled, having given his life to Christ, and he returns to the light. He walks towards the ship. The mast of the vessel is the cross; the sail of the boat represents the blood-stained body of Jesus. In Christianity, a ship is a symbol of the church. Through the work of Christ, the man in blue will board the ship and return home to the Father.

The man in the painting has reversed his direction. He has transitioned from the man in red to the man in blue. By faith, he moves towards the light. Christ,

and his words enable our lives to change direction. Eugene Peterson's translation of 2 Corinthians 3:18 reminds us, "And so we are transfigured much like the Messiah, our lives gradually becoming brighter and more beautiful as God enters our lives and we become like him."

We will now move into the great reversal study.

The Penitent Thief

Luke 23:39-43 (ESV)

[39] One of the criminals who were hanged railed at him, saying, "Are you not the Christ? Save yourself and us!" [40] But the other rebuked him, saying, "Do you not fear God, since you are under the same sentence of condemnation? [41] And we indeed justly, for we are receiving the due reward of our deeds; but this man has done nothing wrong." [42] And he said, "Jesus, remember me when you come into your kingdom." [43] And he said to him, "Truly, I say to you, today you will be with me in paradise."

Christ and the Good Thief
Titian

Jesus is being crucified. Hours earlier, when Judas betrayed Jesus in the garden of Gethsemane, the disciples forsook Christ and fled. Next, Peter denied Jesus three times. At the crucifixion, best case, John was "nearby," and the other disciples looked on from "a distance." After the crucifixion, the disciples are huddled up together behind locked doors. *Dear Jesus, are you sure you picked the right group of guys to be your disciples?*

Back to the crucifixion.

The repentant criminal, crucified next to Jesus, speaking in the passage from Luke above, is sometimes referred to as Dismas. He was a criminal, a malefactor, a doer of evil. He was sentenced to death. Dismas was at the bottom of the first-century Palestinian ecosystem.

On the cross, next to Jesus, something remarkable happened. Dismas confessed his sin and declared Jesus to be innocent. Next, he gave us the first direct indication of faith in the dying Messiah. Amazing. The disciples, who Jesus has spent the last three years of his life with, have betrayed him, denied him, or fled from him. They had the benefit of our Lord's instruction. As far as we know, Dismas did not. And yet, this half-dead, corrupt man surged forward in faith to rely on the grace of Christ. Very shortly, Dismas will find that he is not in Kansas anymore.

James Burton Coffman gives us a unique insight in his commentary on Luke 23:40. "One corollary of the soul's awareness of God's presence is the accompanying recognition of one's own unworthiness; and upon this premise, it is safe to conclude that the Penitent Thief had recognized God himself in the person of Jesus Christ the Lord." [3]

The Penitent Thief is a Christian mandala I created over a long period while reflecting on the crucifixion passage in Luke 23. The focus of the image comes from verse 43, where Jesus tells the penitent thief on the cross next to him that he would be with our Lord in paradise that day.

The Penitent Thief
Kerry Pierce

The image is surreal, disorienting at first, but it entices us to ask questions and explore.

The lower hand is that of the penitent criminal in Luke 23. This criminal, crucified next to Jesus, is sometimes referred to as Dismas. The middle hand is that of the second thief crucified next to Jesus. Finally, the top hand is Jesus'.

Dismas was a criminal, a malefactor, a doer of evil. Sentenced to death, Dismas was at the bottom of the first-century Palestinian society.

On the cross, next to Jesus, something remarkable happened. Dismas confessed his sin and declared Jesus to be innocent. Next, he gave us the first direct expression of faith in the dying Messiah. This half-dead, corrupt man, surged forward in faith to rely on the grace of Christ.

This moment is summarized in the mandala with the drop of blood the fell from the hand of Christ. The second thief chooses to allow the blood of Christ to pass him by. The believing, repentant Dismas reaches out to receive Christ's blood.

Made clean by his faith in Christ's work, Dismas joined Jesus in paradise.

Despite his background, Dismas believed in Jesus, and he was saved. Dismas, almost literally, made his decision for Christ at the last minute.

A great reversal.

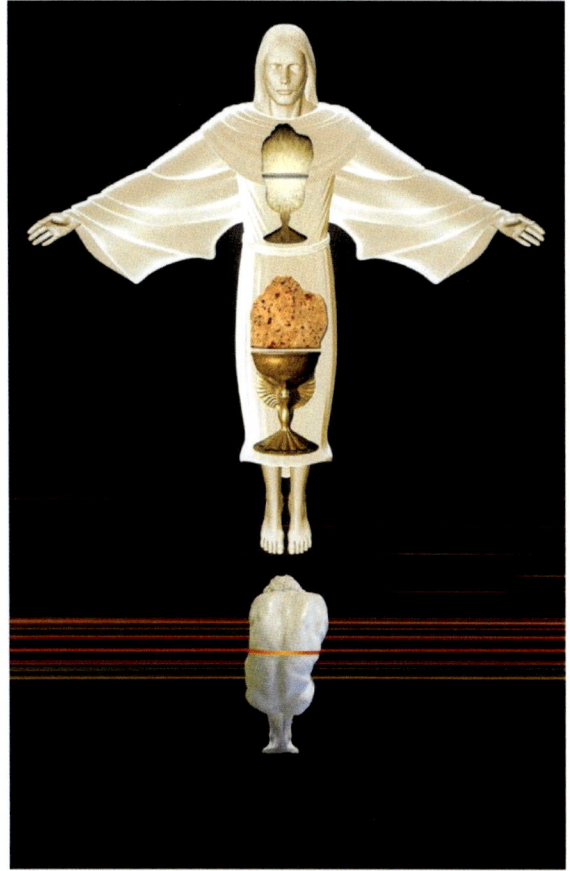

Humility and Repentance

The Pharisee and the Tax Collector

Luke 18:9-14

[9]He [Jesus] also told this parable to some who trusted in themselves that they were righteous, and treated others with contempt: [10]"Two men went up into the temple to pray, one a Pharisee and the other a tax collector. [11]The Pharisee, standing by himself, prayed thus: 'God, I thank you that I am not like other men, extortioners, unjust, adulterers, or even like this tax collector. [12]I fast twice a week; I give tithes of all that I get.' [13]But the tax collector, standing far off, would not even lift up his eyes to heaven, but beat his breast, saying, 'God, be merciful to me, a sinner!' [14]I tell you, this man went down to his house justified, rather than the other. For everyone who exalts himself will be humbled, but the one who humbles himself will be exalted."

The story is moving along, and then the last verse comes out of Jesus' mouth. The first-century Palestinian audience had their reality shattered. Some may have walked away disgusted; others gained new insight.

A modern engineer, unfamiliar with first-century Palestinian culture, would ask for context to understand the story.

The two men Jesus brings together in this story are very different in the minds of the listening audience.

The Pharisee would have been highly respected by other Jews. The Jewish tax collector would be at the other end of the cultural respect scale. He would have been considered a traitor: a man who collected taxes from his own people and then gave the money to the non-Jewish ruling authorities while keeping any excess funds for himself.

Like the Penitent Thief, the tax collector is near the bottom of the first-century Palestinian ecosystem.

For everyone who exalts himself will be humbled, but the one who humbles himself will be exalted.

Recall the phrase, "tax collectors and sinners." These two categories are lumped together throughout Matthew, Mark, and Luke.

In the parable, both men pray. The surprise comes. Jesus declares the repentant, humble tax collector to be in the right. The pronouncement by Jesus is shocking in its original context. Jesus has turned the expectations of the first-century Palestinian audience upside down.

The error of the Pharisee in the parable is that he thinks he can be obedient to God while having disdain for others.

The first-century culture's value system distances the two men. We discover that Jesus distances them by a different metric—spiritual poverty and humility versus self-righteousness and pride. Jesus discards the cultural context of the day and replaces it with God's context.

Cultural expectations are upset, providing another reminder that God's standards may often be radically different than culture's standards.

Repentance is an act of humility. One becomes aware of their sin. We turn and confess them to Christ. As Christ was merciful to the Penitent Thief, he shows mercy in his forgiveness to repentant sinners.

Christ is our standard. We study the Bible; we chew on the Word of God, applying it to our lives. We pray. With time we become more and more Christ-like. As we consider Christ and our own sin, we are humbled. A humble heart is a good soil that God will use to bear fruit for the Kingdom. "Blessed are the poor in spirit." In the process, we become more obedient to God, and we grow in our love of God and our neighbor.

Again, consider Jesus. In John 13, we find him washing the feet of his disciples. Foot washing is the work of slaves. The Son of God is giving the disciples a lesson in humility. Christian discipleship is humility. The theologian Frederick Dale Bruner notes: "There is no parallel in ancient literature for a person of superior status voluntarily washing the feet

Jesus Washing Peter's Feet
Ford Madox Brown

of someone of inferior status."[4]

And again, consider Jesus. In Luke 2:16, we find Jesus, born in a manger visited by shepherds. First, one of the most far-reaching events in history occurs in a structure built for animals. Our Lord is born homeless. Shepherds then visit the Christ-child. From his excellent commentary on Luke, Robert Stein tells us, "In general shepherds were dishonest and unclean according to the standards of the law. They represent the outcasts and sinners for whom Jesus came. Such outcasts were the first recipients of the good news."[5]

Jesus was obedient and humble, and Jesus is exalted.

Spiritual leadership. As of this writing, the attendance of Willow Creek Community Church in Chicago averages 26 thousand on a given weekend. One of the executive Pastors was nagged by questions: Are we helping people become more Christ-like? Are they growing in their love for God and others? The leadership surveyed their congregation. The results were disappointing. Eighteen percent of the congregation had stalled spiritually. Many were considering leaving. The team went on to survey over 1,000 churches, over 250,000 congregants.

The research found that in the top 5% of churches, churches where the congregants were growing in their love for God and others, the leaders were disarmingly humble.[6] Humble disciples of Christ bear good fruit for the Kingdom

Unexpected by the world's standards, but God gives grace to the humble and exalts them.

The image shown was rendered by the French artist James Tissot. It is entitled *The Pharisee and the Publican*. Tissot's work is a straightforward Biblical illustration of Jesus' story.

Tissot was a prodigal son. Returning to the Catholic faith late in life, Tissot spent much of the remainder of his life painting a series of 350 watercolors illustrating the life of Christ. Shortly after his return to faith, Tissot visited the Holy Land

The Pharisee and the Publican
James Tissot

to record the region's landscape, architecture, clothing, and customs before the introduction of the railroad. His illustrations provide a large body of work, giving us a window into the earthly life and time of Jesus.

The Last are First, and the First are Last
Reversal

Luke 13:22-30

[22] He went on his way through towns and villages, teaching and journeying toward Jerusalem. [23] And someone said to him, "Lord, will those who are saved be few?" And he said to them, [24] "Strive to enter through the narrow door. For many, I tell you, will seek to enter and will not be able. [25] When once the master of the house has risen and shut the door, and you begin to stand outside and to knock at the door, saying, 'Lord, open to us,' then he will answer you, 'I do not know where you come from.' [26] Then you will begin to say, 'We ate and drank in your presence, and you taught in our streets.' [27] But he will say, 'I tell you, I do not know where you come from. Depart from me, all you workers of evil!' [28] In that place there will be weeping and gnashing of teeth when you see Abraham and Isaac and Jacob and all the prophets in the kingdom of God but you yourselves cast out. [29] And people will come from east and west, and from north and south, and recline at table in the kingdom of God. [30] And behold, some are last who will be first, and some are first who will be last."

And behold,

some are last

who will be first,

and some are first

who will be last.

On the way to Jerusalem, someone asks Jesus, "...will those who are saved be few?" Luke doesn't tell us who inquired. The question does have the feel of a query designed to test Jesus. If Jesus says a few, he's possibly too strict, and if he says everyone, he makes salvation cheap.

Jesus doesn't answer the question directly. His response is shocking, challenging those listening then, and us today, to ask ourselves if we will enter into God's kingdom.

Jesus is the master of the house.

The Messianic Banquet refers to God's kingdom.

Entrance through the narrow door into the Kingdom is granted to repentant individuals. Individuals who believe in the work Christ did on our behalf. The Penitent Thief is a good example.

The "you" in verse 26 refers to the Jewish elite, aka, "the first." The reference especially calls to mind the Pharisees and the rich ruler. The people from the east, west, north, and south refer to gentiles, the outcasts, the tax collectors, sinners, shepherds, penitent thieves, and the poor, aka "the last." Note the time element; the door will close after a time.

The summary is that many of the world's first, who expect to enter into God's kingdom, will be excluded, becoming the last by the Kingdom's standards. Many of the world's last, who are expected to be excluded by the world, will become the first by the Kingdom's standards.

Christians today are reminded that we do not gain entrance to the Kingdom based upon who our parents are, what church committees we served on, or our worldly status and titles. We fix our eyes on Jesus' standards rather than the world's standards. Like the tax collector in Luke 18, we humbly repent. Like the Penitent Thief in Luke 23, we place our faith in Christ. It is our response to Jesus that matters.

The Great Metaphysician
Georgio de Chirico

The image shown is de Chirico's painting, *The Great Metaphysician.* *The Great Metaphysician* is reminiscent of Tissot's illustration, *The Pharisee and the Publican.* We begin with the tall central statue dominating the center of the composition. The lower portion of the figure is constructed of wood and cloth elements. At the top of the statue is a faceless plaster bust.

When we Christianize the painting, the bust represents those who are first in this world. Elevated in status and firmly grounded in the world. This individual is somewhat reminiscent of the Pharisee in Luke 18.

But the statue is empty inside. We see an unusual element in the center of the figure, which projects the image's background to the front of the statue. The proud plaster head at the top of the structure is faceless. This individual is elevated but lacks the eyes to see spiritually. They represent the first who will become the last because they are spiritually blind. Spiritually blind and unable to see, much less pass through, the small open door at the right of the image.

A modest individual stands to the left of the open door. This individual can see the door and move through it. Small by the world's standards, the humble, repentant individual will pass through the entrance to the Messianic Banquet. Even though he cannot see where the door will lead, he moves forward into the Kingdom by faith. This individual reminds us of the tax collector in Luke 18.

In the image, the shadows are long. It is late in the day, and there are no artificial lights. When night comes, it will no longer be possible to locate the door.

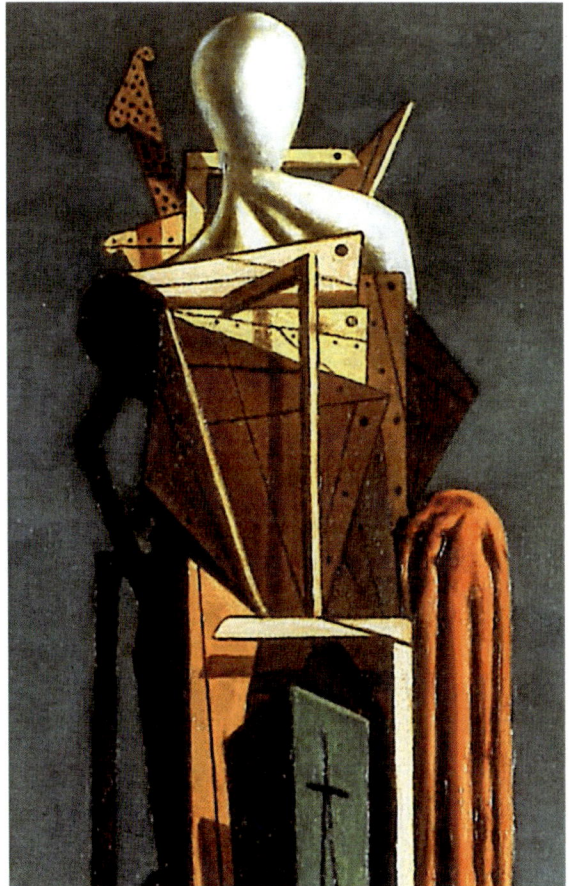

Childlike Trust

Luke 18:15-17

[15] Now they were bringing even infants to him that he might touch them. And when the disciples saw it, they rebuked them. [16] But Jesus called them to him, saying, "Let the children come to me, and do not hinder them, for to such belongs the kingdom of God. [17] Truly, I say to you, whoever does not receive the kingdom of God like a child shall not enter it."

A little later in Luke 18, Jesus will remind his disciples that they are on their way to Jerusalem, where he will be put to death. You have to admire this God-man who would take time to bless infants while on his way to the Cross.

The Song of Love
Georgio de Chirico

The painting shown is entitled *The Song of Love*. The image, like Jesus' saying, "whoever does not receive the kingdom of God like a child shall not enter it," is unexpected and perhaps disorienting. It is best to explore the image with a sense of childlike curiosity.

De Chirico painted *The Song of Love* in 1914. This work often appears in books on Surrealist Painting, even though de Chirico rendered the image a decade before André Breton's 1924 *Surrealist Manifesto*.[7]

Two realms again. In the first realm, we have the plaster head of Apollo, a surgeon's glove, a cloth ball, and architectural elements. In this realm, the items are three-dimensional, casting shadows. An unexplained light source illuminates the bottom of the ball. In the second realm, we have a black component and a white cloud-like element. This area could be read as depicting a train engine or perhaps a factory. In this realm, the structures are two-dimensional; that is, they look flat.

Again, I will take de Chirico's meaning and Christianize it.

The first realm is the world. The plaster head of Apollo is the god of this realm. He stands above everything else, the largest, the brightest, the most beautiful element in the domain, gazing off with no concern other than his handsome appearance. Apollo, in this context, represents the illusion of pride.

Staying in the realm of the world, we next come to the surgeon's glove. This element symbolizes birth into the world.

The ball symbolizes a child, or specifically, the children Jesus refers to in Luke 18.

A child has been born into the world with the assistance of a doctor. The child comes to rest below the prideful Apollo, who does not have time to acknowledge the child's existence. The contrast is created. The prideful Apollo stands above all else in his realm, and the humble child is positioned below him.

The second realm, the background, is different. Its two-dimensional nature separates it from the first realm, as does the brick wall. The capacity for movement further differentiates the domains. The head of Apollo and the surgeon's glove are fastened tightly to the world. Interpreting the dark element as a train gives the second realm capacity for motion. The second realm symbolizes the kingdom of God.

Finally, the ball, representing the humble, trusting child, is capable of movement. It is the one element in the first realm capable of easily moving from the first realm to the second realm. The ball is not held in place by pride or position.

The second light source illuminating the ball from below causes the ball to appear less three-dimensional. That is, its appearance is more two-dimensional, like the elements in the second realm. This light opposes the darkness of the shadow cast by the ball. The second light, the light of Christ, enables a childlike quality in the ball. By embracing the light and opposing the darkness, the ball possesses the properties that allow it to enter the second realm. The childlike ball will be first in the Kingdom; the prideful Apollo will be last.

What are the qualities of a child that Jesus considers Kingdom worthy?

Trust. It's a warm summer day. My daughter Kirsten and I are standing in the water at the edge of a lake. Kirsten, who was about two and a half years old at the time, is up to her belly button in the crystal clear water.

I've got a dozen or so small, flat, smooth stones. The kind of rocks that are perfect for skipping across the smooth surface of a lake. Rather than learning how to skim stones across the water, Kirsten takes the rocks one by one and slides them carefully into the water so she can watch their motion as they flutter down to her feet.

Suddenly Kirsten slips and falls into the water. Because the underwater profile of the lake fell off sharply, when she stood up, her head was below water. Kirsten had never been wholly submerged at this point in her life. From under the water, she looked directly into my eyes. The expression on her face is completely calm. There is no fear in her eyes. She merely lifts her right arm upward through the water's surface to me so that I can lift her out of the water. A young girl's childlike trust in her father.

At age 12, I still had elements of childlike trust in my parents. I knew there would be food on the table, a house to return to, and a vehicle to take me places my bike couldn't readily reach. I didn't give any thought to these things. I knew I wasn't in control and trusted that my parents were. The farthest I thought ahead was to the next recess period.

At 12, there was humility. My recklessness led to mistakes. However, at my core, there was a desire to be obedient to my parents, a belief that they still knew more than I did. I was to obey them rather than have them obey me.

Finally, there was and continues to be curiosity. As John Medina writes in his book, *Brain Rules*, "The greatest Brain Rule of all is something I cannot prove or characterize, but I believe in it with all my heart. As my son was trying to tell me, it is the importance of curiosity."[8] Curiosity, a childlike belief that I don't know everything about God and that I want to spend my life learning more and more. Medina goes on to write, "Babies are the model of how we learn – not by passive reaction to the environment but by active testing through observation, hypotheses, experiment, and conclusion."[9]

William Barclay writes, "To keep alive the sense of wonder, to live in unquestioning trust, instinctively to obey, to forgive and to forget – that is the childlike spirit, and that is the passport to the kingdom of God" [10]

Like the tax collector in the prior passage of Luke 18, we add repentance.

Contrast this with pride. The prideful individual needs to be obeyed; needs to be served; needs to always be in the right; knows everything already, and believes they do not need forgiveness. They trust in themselves.

Embrace childlike trust in Jesus, receive the Kingdom, and be blessed.

Rich Toward God

Luke 12:16-21

[16] And he told them a parable, saying, "The land of a rich man produced plentifully, [17] and he thought to himself, 'What shall I do, for I have nowhere to store my crops?' [18] And he said, 'I will do this: I will tear down my barns and build larger ones, and there I will store all my grain and my goods. [19] And I will say to my soul, "Soul, you have ample goods laid up for many years; relax, eat, drink, be merry."' [20] But God said to him, 'Fool! This night your soul is required of you, and the things you have prepared, whose will they be?' [21] So is the one who lays up treasure for himself and is not rich toward God."

"I will…, I will…, I will…." The rich man was blessed with plentiful crops. His reaction was to think of himself.

The Man Who Hoards
James Tissot

Tissot's painting, *The Man Who Hoards,* shows a wealthy man reclined amid his harvest of plenty. Dressed lavishly, surrounded by enough food to feed a small village, his posture is suggestive of his self-centered mindset. Externally, he is the picture of success. God's verdict is that the man is a fool.

Tissot's composition includes an angel holding a sword behind the rich man. The image suggests that the man's physical life, and his plans for it, are about to come to an immediate end.

I knew a brilliant engineering manager named David. A gifted mind, technical vision, and drive led him to the position of Chief Technology Officer of a long-standing semiconductor company. He was reported to be in excellent health. At age 62, he died suddenly during his morning workout. He died one day before his scheduled retirement. Heartbreaking. Even the brightest minds among us are not in complete control of their lives. Fortunately, because of his upcoming retirement, other employees in the company had a chance to share their appreciation and well wishes with David.

The parable of the Rich Fool and the sudden, unfortunate death of David cause us to reflect. Right now, which future am I investing in, my worldly future or my heavenly future? For those considering retirement, how will you use your time, energy, and resources going forward? For all of us who claim to be disciples of Christ, are we investing in the Kingdom or ourselves?

The parable of the Rich Fool reminds us that what is invested with God is permanent. What is invested in earthly possessions is temporary.

For those approaching retirement age, the parable is especially challenging. Perhaps you are closing in on age 65. The questions begin to circle in one's mind. Do you have enough savings to enjoy a comfortable retirement? For folks in this position, faith in God becomes a daily reality. How much do I keep in savings versus how much do I invest in God's kingdom?

We receive the Kingdom with childlike trust. After receiving the Kingdom, disciples continue to trust in Christ.

The parable tells us that life is not about our plans for security. Discipleship is about how we use our wealth, be it large or small. Dad once taught in a sermon that how we use our possessions and our time reveals who we are.

Dear Jesus, this is challenging. It goes against our cultural norms. We protest. We want to control our future. Who will take care of us if we don't take care of ourselves? Jesus' answer throughout Luke 12 is "do not fear." A few verses later in Luke, chapter 12, Jesus gives us assurance.

Luke 12:32-34

[32] "Fear not, little flock, for it is your Father's good pleasure to give you the kingdom. [33] Sell your possessions, and give to the needy. Provide yourselves with moneybags that do not grow old, with a treasure in the heavens that does not fail, where no thief approaches and no moth destroys. [34] For where your treasure is, there will your heart be also.

Jesus urges us to use our earthly possessions in this life to build for the Kingdom.

Again, Tissot became a Christian later in life. He spent the later years of his life using his gifts to illustrate the New Testament, leaving behind a body of work that benefits the Christian community today. Tissot intentionally painted *The Man Who Hoards* to depict Jesus' parable of the Rich Fool.

De Chirico's painting, *The Enigma of the Oracle,* was not intended to illustrate Jesus' parable, but it is very effective in doing so. The work is a very early painting in de Chirico's career. My reading of the image is probably not precisely aligned with de Chirico's original intentions. In other words, I hope to Christianize the meaning of the image without straying too far from Giorgio's original intentions.

For where

your treasure is,

there

will your heart

be also.

The Enigma of the Oracle
Georgio de Chirico

As with many de Chirico paintings, there are two realms. The region on the left represents the world. The world is bright, clouds move, the sky is blue, and waves break in. There is movement and life. The region on the right represents the individual's investment in the Kingdom. The curtain represents the Holy of Holies, the area in the Old Testament tabernacle where the very presence of God abides. The curtain remains closed, and the face of God does not shine upon the emptiness in the architectural area beyond the curtain.

Most importantly, there is a temporal juxtaposition—earthy life and eternity.

The single solitary figure with her back to us is at the precarious point where the two realms overlap. For a moment, she occupies both domains. The wind blows the curtain in front of her outward, perhaps representing her last earthly breath.

The figure looks back over the world she has so profoundly embraced. It is a world where her hedonistic life was played out. There are bigger barns in the image. We see homes, and summer homes, and timeshares. Behind the individual is the sum of the treasure she has laid up for the Kingdom of heaven. There is nothing. She contemplates the emptiness of her soul.

The individual is re-thinking her life from the spiritual perspective now. It is too late.

Jesus assures us that if we seek God's kingdom, our Father's good pleasure is to give it to us. Let it be our good pleasure to put our treasure in that kingdom.

35

Prodigal Son, aka, The Compassionate Father and His Two Lost Sons

Luke 15:11-32

The Return of the Prodigal Son
Rembrandt

¹¹ And he said, "There was a man who had two sons. ¹² And the younger of them said to his father, 'Father, give me the share of property that is coming to me.' And he divided his property between them. ¹³ Not many days later, the younger son gathered all he had and took a journey into a far country, and there he squandered his property in reckless living. ¹⁴ And when he had spent everything, a severe famine arose in that country, and he began to be in need. ¹⁵ So he went and hired himself out to one of the citizens of that country, who sent him into his fields to feed pigs. ¹⁶ And he was longing to be fed with the pods that the pigs ate, and no one gave him anything.

¹⁷ "But when he came to himself, he said, 'How many of my father's hired servants have more than enough bread, but I perish here with hunger! ¹⁸ I will arise and go to my father, and I will say to him, "Father, I have sinned against heaven and before you. ¹⁹ I am no longer worthy to be called your son. Treat me as one of your hired servants."' ²⁰ And he arose and came to his father. But while he was still a long way off, his father saw him and felt compassion, and ran and embraced him and kissed him. ²¹ And the son said to him, 'Father, I have sinned against heaven and before you. I am no longer worthy to be called your son.' ²² But the father said to his servants, 'Bring quickly the best robe, and put it on him, and put a ring on his hand, and shoes on his feet. ²³ And bring the fattened calf and kill it, and let us eat and celebrate. ²⁴ For this my son was dead, and is alive again; he was lost, and is found.' And they began to celebrate.

²⁵ "Now his older son was in the field, and as he came and drew near to the house, he heard music and dancing. ²⁶ And he called one of the servants and

asked what these things meant. ²⁷ And he said to him, 'Your brother has come, and your father has killed the fattened calf, because he has received him back safe and sound.' ²⁸ But he was angry and refused to go in. His father came out and entreated him, ²⁹ but he answered his father, 'Look, these many years I have served you, and I never disobeyed your command, yet you never gave me a young goat, that I might celebrate with my friends. ³⁰ But when this son of yours came, who has devoured your property with prostitutes, you killed the fattened calf for him!' ³¹ And he said to him, 'Son, you are always with me, and all that is mine is yours. ³² It was fitting to celebrate and be glad, for this your brother was dead, and is alive; he was lost, and is found.'"

The Prodigal Son's behavior was bad. Seriously bad.

Hearing the parable from Jesus' lips, the first-century Palestinian audience may have recalled Deuteronomy 21: 18 – 21.

¹⁸ "If a man has a stubborn and rebellious son who will not obey the voice of his father or the voice of his mother, and, though they discipline him, will not listen to them, ¹⁹ then his father and his mother shall take hold of him and bring him out to the elders of his city at the gate of the place where he lives, ²⁰ and they shall say to the elders of his city, 'This our son is stubborn and rebellious; he will not obey our voice; he is a glutton and a drunkard.' ²¹ Then all the men of the city shall stone him to death with stones. So you shall purge the evil from your midst, and all Israel shall hear, and fear."

Ouch.

The Prodigal Son took his inheritance early, left home, and engaged in reckless living. Or, as the KJV version translates it, "riotous living." The rich fool of Luke 12 thought about using his abundance to eat, drink and be merry. The Prodigal Son put the rich man's thoughts into action. He used his possessions

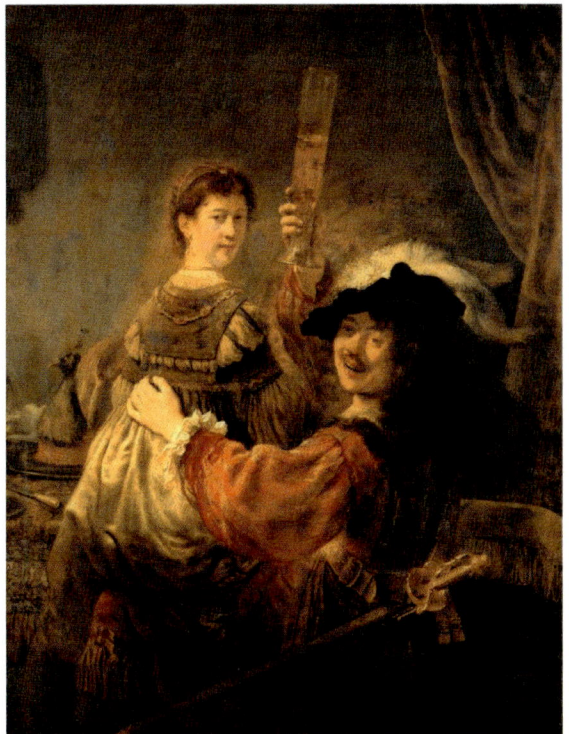

The Prodigal Son in a Tavern
Rembrandt

The Return of the Prodigal Son
James Tissot

foolishly.

The son repents. He repents and decides to return to his father.

The father receives his son with compassion and with joy. Great joy. The eager father initiates an extravagant celebration.

Summing up. The son takes his share of the family inheritance, leaves his family, and parties until his share of the family property is gone. He repents and goes home. On returning, he finds no condemnation but rather a party celebrating his return. Lost and found. A great reversal.

The father's attitude and actions are unexpected and beautiful.

The parable then contrasts the father's attitude of celebration with the older son's disdain. The perspectives of the father and the older son are reversed.

Prodigal sons and daughters, know that you have a heavenly Father who longs for your return. You have a savior who associated with sinners to bring them to repentance. Jesus transformed Matthew from being a traitor and tax-collector into a disciple. With God, we rejoice at the repentant sinner's return.

Prodigal Son – Georgio de Chirico

De Chirico's painting *The Prodigal Son* features a mannequin and a statue, two abstractions of the human form. Both are artificial.

The Prodigal Son
Georgio de Chirico

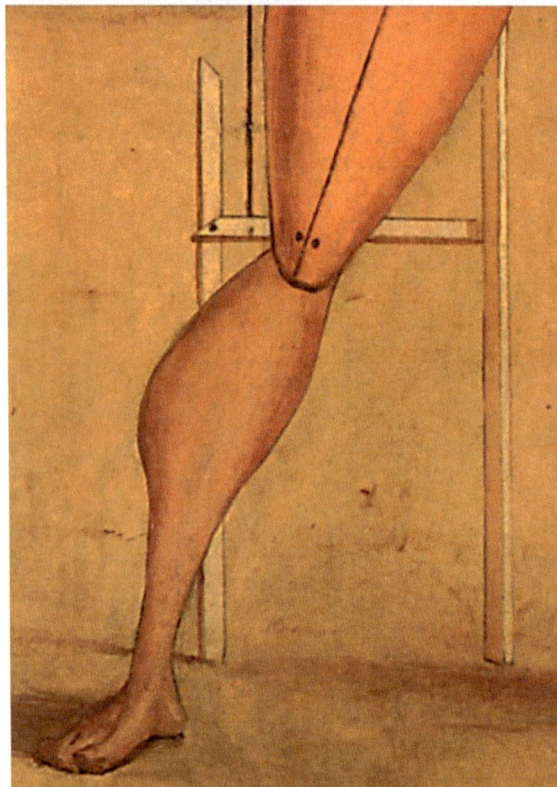

So far, we have looked at works from what is considered de Chirico's metaphysical period, dating from 1909 to 1919. After 1919 de Chirico works in a more "classic" or neo-classical style. However, from 1922 to 1930, de Chirico produced paintings connected to his earlier metaphysical period. The Prodigal Son, painted in 1922, provides an excellent example of a work that crosses over between the two styles.

For de Chirico, the father is the plaster or stone statue that calls to mind the art of classical antiquity. The mannequin is the son.

De Chirico is using the mannequin to project himself, autobiographically, into his art. The mannequin is painted in the metaphysical style representing de Chirico himself during that period of his life. As a painter, he is the metaphysical son returning to the classic father. The image captures the evolution of de Chirico's artistic style.

Let's examine de Chirico's *The Prodigal Son* again, but from a Christian perspective.

Again, the statue represents the father. The father was positioned at a high location to look for the son's return and lowered himself from the pedestal. The figure has given up its place of honor on the pedestal in the lower right corner of the painting. The property of mobility is added to the statue, a feature that enables the figure to embrace his returning son.

The mannequin, again, represents the Prodigal Son. At first, the son appears to be large and muscular, having traveled from the distant land in the background. As we look closer at the son, we see that he is broken. Composed of artificial forms which have been screwed together, the son needs support to stand. Scaffolding built from stretcher bars, set squares, and other elements hold him in position. The son has only one arm. His missing right arm has been replaced with weights to help him maintain balance.

Saddest of all, the son is faceless. His identity is almost lost.

The Christ has come down from heaven to reach out and embrace sinful humanity and give us back our identities. The returning son is repentant, exposing his sin to the Christ. The son is forgiven.

Prodigal Sons

The Prodigal Son has taken different personalities throughout time. Notable prodigal sons include Rembrandt, James Tissot, Salvador Dali, Alice Cooper, Stephen Baldwin, and others. With the artists that become believers later in life, one notes a transformation in their work. Both Rembrandt and Tissot rendered paintings of the Prodigal Son. More than once.

The Return of the Prodigal Son
James Tissot

The Giving and Receiving Reversal

Acts 20:35

It is more

blessed to give

than to receive.

"In all things I have shown you that by working hard in this way we must help the weak and remember the words of the Lord Jesus, how he himself said, 'It is more blessed to give than to receive.'"

As a boy, my mother used to tell me that it was "more blessed to give than to receive." Her instruction fell into the same category as "eat your Brussel sprouts; they are really good for you." Growing up, I didn't buy into either assertion. Fortunately, mother's wisdom was not lost.

The Apostle Paul worked a day job. By trade, he was a tentmaker, performing manual work. He worked hard, giving himself to the work of the Gospel.

Though the saying "It is more blessed to give than to receive" sounds backward, the phrase makes sense from the Kingdom's perspective. From 2 Corinthians 9:6, "The point is this: whoever sows sparingly will also reap sparingly, and whoever sows bountifully will also reap bountifully." Or, as the Hawai'i Pidgin translation renders the text, "But I tell you guys dis: 'Da guy who plant litto bit seed, he goin get one small crop. Da guy dat plant plenny seed wit good heart, he goin get mo plenny crop, an he goin stay good inside.'"

Sometimes our day jobs are challenging, but our work puts many of us into a position where we can give to others, blessing them out of our abundance.

To bless and promote the happiness of others out of pure motive is a beautiful action. As disciples, we do this for others, for Christ, and to Christ.

Consider the words of Christ in Matthew 25:34-40:

³⁴ "Then the King will say to those on his right, 'Come, you who are blessed by my Father, inherit the kingdom prepared for you from the foundation of the world. ³⁵ For I was hungry and you gave me food, I was thirsty and you gave me drink, I was a stranger and you welcomed me, ³⁶ I was naked and you clothed me, I was sick and you visited me, I was in prison and you came to me.' ³⁷ Then the righteous will answer him, saying, 'Lord, when did we see you hungry and feed you, or thirsty and give you drink? ³⁸ And when did we see you a stranger and welcome you, or naked and clothe you? ³⁹ And when did we see you sick or in prison and visit you?' ⁴⁰ And the King will answer them, 'Truly, I say to you, as you did it to one of the least of these my brothers, you did it to me.'"

The best examples of giving, rather than receiving, come from our Lord. Consider de Chirico's work *Vendredi Saint* or *Holy Friday*. The most disorienting thing about this image is that de Chirico painted it. The work is full of textbook Christian symbolism rendered by an individual who did not profess Christianity. *Giorgio, what were you thinking?*

Why Giorgio de Chirico painted *Holy Friday* is a bit of a mystery. De Chirico was friends with another painter named Carlo Carrà, who was a Christian; however, this friendship didn't begin until after the painting of *Holy Friday*. Research indicates that Jean Cocteau, the French artist and filmmaker who bought that painting, was also the person who gave the work its title. Cocteau was a Christian and an artist. Hence the Christian symbolism would have resonated with him leading him to provide the image with a name of Christian significance. It is possible that Cocteau requested de Chirico to render the image.

The composition is from the perspective of a staging or storage room located just off of a church sanctuary. In the background are familiar architectural elements. Arches that belong to a vaulted ceiling appear at the top of the composition.

Vendredi Saint
Georgio de Chirico

Towards the center of the image is an altar. The arches forming the ceiling appear to morph into loaves of bread as we move down to the altar. The altar is used to celebrate the Sacrament of Holy Communion, also known as The Lord's Supper. Christians observe the Lord's Supper "in remembrance" of Christ's giving of himself on the Cross.

The apple is a symbol of sin or the fall into sin. The apple on the right would symbolize Adam's fall into sin. The apple between the apple on the right and the egg would represent the work of Christ who took on our sin. The egg is the Christian symbol for the resurrection.

On Good Friday, Jesus, our high priest, became the blood sacrifice and scapegoat for our sins. Our sins are transferred to him, and his righteousness is imputed to us. We are made clean.

Christ, by the act of giving his life for us, blessed us. We received his righteousness. Out of the abundance of who he was, his sinless nature, and his love, he gave himself for us. Indeed, it is more blessed to give than to receive. Imagine if Christ had shown up only to be worshipped as a king and never endured the cross for us. We Christians would not be in the privileged position of being temples of the Holy Spirit. There would be no home for prodigal sons and daughters to come home to. Christ sows bountifully, and he reaps bountifully.

The Good Samaritan Reversal – From Where do Good Neighbors Come?

Luke 10:25-37

[25] And behold, a lawyer stood up to put him to the test, saying, "Teacher, what shall I do to inherit eternal life?" [26] He said to him, "What is written in the Law? How do you read it?" [27] And he answered, "You shall love the Lord your God with all your heart and with all your soul and with all your strength and with all your mind, and your neighbor as yourself." [28] And he said to him, "You have answered correctly; do this, and you will live."

[29] But he, desiring to justify himself, said to Jesus, "And who is my neighbor?" [30] Jesus replied, "A man was going down from Jerusalem to Jericho, and he fell among robbers, who stripped him and beat him and departed, leaving him half dead. [31] Now by chance a priest was going down that road, and when he saw him he passed by on the other side. [32] So likewise a Levite, when he came to the place and saw him, passed by on the other side. [33] But a Samaritan, as he journeyed, came to where he was, and when he saw him, he had compassion. [34] He went to him and bound up his wounds, pouring on oil and wine. Then he set him on his own animal and brought him to an inn and took care of him. [35] And the next day he took out two denarii and gave them to the innkeeper, saying, 'Take care of him, and whatever more you spend, I will repay you when I come back.' [36] Which of these three, do you think, proved to be a neighbor to the man who fell among the robbers?" [37] He said, "The one who showed him mercy." And Jesus said to him, "You go, and do likewise."

The Good Samaritan
Vincent van Gogh

This is another story from Jesus that would have surprised a first-century Palestinian audience.

Dear Jesus, this story is going to rub some people the wrong way.

Again, to understand the story, a modern engineer, unfamiliar with first-century Palestine,

The Good Samaritan
Rembrandt

would ask for context.

Bandits were known to exploit travelers as they made the journey between Jerusalem and Jericho. This road was dangerous.

The traveler who fell among robbers, if he traveled by himself, would have been an easy target.

The priest would be a descendant of Aaron, the older brother of Moses. Aaron was the first High priest. The priest in the parable is a Jewish religious leader who ministers in the temple. He passes by the half-dead traveler.

The Levite is a member of the tribe of Levi, just as Aaron was, but not a descendant of Aaron. He too, is a Jewish religious leader, something of a priest's assistant in the temple. He also passes by the half-dead traveler.

The Samaritan. For a Jew, a Samaritan was not a person to be respected. Jews generally disliked Samaritans.

Again, like the parable of the Pharisee and the Tax Collector, the men Jesus brings together in this story are very different in the minds of the listening audience.

The priest and the Levite would have been highly respected by other Jews. The Samaritan would be at the other end of the cultural respect spectrum. However, it is the Samaritan that fulfills the Mosaic Law. Deuteronomy 6:5 "You shall love the Lord your God with all your heart and with all your soul and with all your might," and Leviticus 19:18b "you shall love your neighbor as yourself." The priest and the Levite fail. A reversal of the listening audience's expectations.

We are neighbors when we discern need and act on it, regardless of who is in need. No boundaries.

Several artists have rendered *Good Samaritan* images, including Van Gogh. I'm showing Tissot's painting of the *Good Samaritan* because it captures what the road from Jerusalem to Jericho might have looked like. Note the rough terrain. In the distance, we see an individual dressed in white, representing either the Priest or the Levite.

The Good Samaritan
James Tissot

The Good Samexicans – Two Cultures Meet

I wave as the black and white police car approaches. The officer doesn't stop to help. Fifteen minutes later, a second police car approaches. Again, it passes without stopping.

I'm standing on the side of the road in San Jose, California, where Interstate 280 crosses over US 101 and turns into Interstate 680. It's the evening rush hour. The fuel pump on my car stopped without any warning, and I am stranded.

A third and fourth police car pass without stopping.

I am a Director at a High Tech startup wearing a custom shirt, tie, slacks, and an expensive pair of Italian shoes. It's the early 1990's, and I don't own a cell phone yet. My ill-fated commute has quickly transformed my situation. I am powerless. My career, my attire, and my job title mean nothing in this environment.

There are eight lanes of commuter traffic, with four moving at the speed limit in my direction, and no one will help me. Over 100 cars per minute are passing me. The police don't stop. I wonder about the 1000s of other people who are passing by in front of me. I wonder if I would pause to help someone out.

I began walking down the bank of dry grass south of the Interstate. Over a rise, I see some homeless men. They stand in groups around 55-gallon drums burning debris to stay warm.

I return to my position at the side of the Interstate. Suddenly a car pulls over and rolls slowly to a stop near me—finally, some help. A pretty Hispanic woman in her early 30s steps out and walks up to me. Maria is out of gas. And then the fun begins.

Within a few minutes, a 1960s Chevy Impala two-door pulls over to pick us up. Maria and I climb into the back seat. Two Mexican men in their early 20s sit in the front of the car. They remind me of Cheech and Chong. I don't intend to be disrespectful. I'm Caucasian. Beyond three years of Spanish in Junior

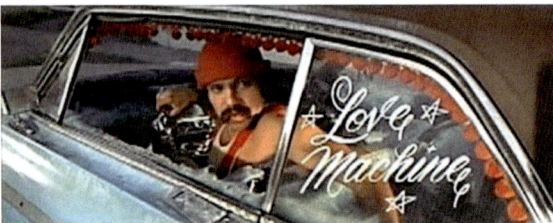

Cheech - 1964 Chevy Impala SS
Paramount Pictures

High, my only glimpse into the Hispanic culture, at that time in my life, was from sitting next to Alice Sanchez in the 3rd grade and listening to the comedy recordings of *Cheech & Chong*.

A conversation begins in Spanish, but the interior of the vehicle overcomes me. It is immaculate. There is shag carpet on the floor and the headliner. Colorful dingle balls decorate the periphery of the windows. Fuzzy dice hang from the rearview mirror. The best element is the chain-link steering wheel.

I like this car.

Maria's laughter jars me out of my admiration of the Hispanic ecosystem I've entered. The two men think Maria and I are married. Maria explains the situation, and the conversation moves to English. After some car talk and a lot of laughter, we arrive at a payphone. The driver gives me change to make the phone call to my wife, and the two good Samaritans wait until they are sure Maria and I will be OK.

Nancy, my wife, picks us up bringing a couple of gallons of gas for Maria. Maria is good to go and gives us her phone number so that she can make dinner for us as a thank-you.

Whenever I read the story of the Good Samaritan, I think of Maria, the two young men, and their car. They gave to me out of their abundance. They saw me as their neighbor; they saw my need, ignored cultural boundaries, and put love into action. Lord, bless them.

Love Your Enemies

Level 1. When Confucius was asked, "Is there one word which may serve as a rule of practice for all one's life?" Confusions answered, "Is not reciprocity such a word? What you do not want done to yourself, do not do to others."

These are good words. If you don't want to be beaten and robbed, don't beat and rob others. Confucius' comments do not preclude actively doing good for another, but reciprocity isn't necessarily a call to action.

Level 2. Leviticus 19:18 states, "You shall not take vengeance or bear a grudge against the sons of your own people, but you shall love your neighbor as yourself: I am the Lord."

Rather than stating the Golden Rule in the negative, the Leviticus text presents the Gold Rule in a positive form. "Love your neighbor as yourself....." Now we have the command to love. Love is a call to action. A call to do good to your neighbor. With the lawyer in the Good Samaritan passage, we ask, "who is my neighbor?" The context of the passage and a narrow interpretation would lead to the conclusion that your neighbor was a fellow Jew, but not a Samaritan, for example.

Level 3. In Luke 6:27a, Jesus states, "But I say to you who hear, Love your enemies...." Jesus exhorts his disciples to love their neighbor regardless of whether they are friends, relatives, or enemies.

Jesus' command is great reversal talk. This is not ordinary love. To love like this is difficult and often goes against human nature. A love that goes beyond reciprocity and is willed into action. The Good Samaritan shows active love to the wounded traveler. Loving one's enemy is appropriate for believers in Christ.

Again, this is a very difficult saying, but it is the love that Christians are called to and made capable of through the work of the Holy Spirit.

Woman at the Well
Carl Bloch

Jesus shares the Gospel with the not so good Samaritan woman at the well

27 "But I say to you who hear, Love your enemies, do good to those who hate you, 28 bless those who curse you, pray for those who abuse you. 29 To one who strikes you on the cheek, offer the other also, and from one who takes away your cloak do not withhold your tunic either. 30 Give to everyone who begs from you, and from one who takes away your goods do not demand them back. 31 And as you wish that others would do to you, do so to them.

32 "If you love those who love you, what benefit is that to you? For even sinners love those who love them. 33 And if you do good to those who do good to you, what benefit is that to you? For even sinners do the same. 34 And if you lend to those from whom you expect to receive, what credit is that to you? Even sinners lend to sinners, to get back the same amount. 35 But love your enemies, and do good, and lend, expecting nothing in return, and your reward will be great, and you will be sons of the Most High, for he is kind to the ungrateful and the evil. 36 Be merciful, even as your Father is merciful."

Your enemies: love, do good, bless and pray for them. *Dear Lord, this is not going to be easy to pull off.*

To love your enemies is to become more and more like Christ. Saul of Tarsus was an enemy. An enemy who breathed threats and murder against the disciples of the Lord, as we are told in Acts 9:1. Jesus reaches out to Saul, the enemy of Christians. Saul was transformed by Christ's love and became Saint Paul, "a servant of Jesus Christ." Again, we see in Paul the effect that Christ's love and mercy have on individual lives.

As disciples, Paul reminds us in Romans 5:8-10 that, "8 God shows his love for us in that while we were still sinners, Christ died for us. 9 Since, therefore, we have now been justified by his blood, much more shall we be saved by him from the wrath of God. 10 For if while we were enemies we were reconciled to God by the death of his Son, much more, now that we are reconciled, shall we be saved

Crucifixion, Seen from the Cross
James Tissot

Father, forgive them,
for they know not what they do

by his life." While we were still enemies, Christ undertook his work to enable us to be reconciled to him. His work on the cross and his words of life have the power to change us from enemies into loving servants of the Kingdom.

Do good to those who hate you. To do good to those who hate us is not a passive attitude. This too, is a call to action. The command is not about feeling; it is about doing. It may take the form of encouraging an enemy towards Christ. The appeal involves actively thinking of the other person's highest good, Christ. For example, in my journey to Christ, pastors and teachers, who thought in terms of my highest good, did not encourage sin in my life. Instead, they pointed me to Scripture and explained Scripture to me. As a result, my behavior became more Christ-like over time; I grew in my relationship with God, and I became much better at discerning his will for my life.

Bless those that curse you. Darrell Bock, in his excellent commentary on Luke, states, "The idea of a blessing is to invoke God's favor on another's behalf or at least appeal to God for that person."[11] In Luke 23:34 Jesus, as he is being put to death, appeals for his enemies saying, "Father, forgive them, for they know not what they do." Again, in Acts 7:60, as Stephen is being stoned to death, he cries out with a loud voice, "Lord do not hold this sin against them."

Pray for those who abuse you. For me, this is a belief that even those who abuse and insult me are not beyond God's reach. I pray for them in the hope that they will find Christ, and in doing so, their lives will be transformed. Praying for those who abuse me is very doable, and it changes my attitude towards the individual when I pray for them. I remind myself of the hope that there is a Saint Paul inside of every Saul I encounter.

If you commute to and from work, you will likely encounter hate, abuse, and possibly some cursing. Love, do good, bless, and pray. To deal with these commute-time scenarios, it is helpful to memorize 1 Corinthians 13:4-7.

Jesus Counsels Nicodemus
William Hole

Jesus shares the Gospel
with Nicodemus, a Pharisee,
who comes
to Jesus by night

[4] Love is patient and kind; love does not envy or boast; it is not arrogant [5]or rude. It does not insist on its own way; it is not irritable or resentful; [6] it does not rejoice at wrongdoing, but rejoices with the truth. [7] Love bears all things, believes all things, hopes all things, endures all things.

De Chirico's painting, *The Enigma of the Hour*, captures an example of the level 3 love to which Jesus calls us. A level of love that calls disciples to love their enemies actively. With this image, I will depart further from de Chirico's original intention as I Christianize the work.

The Engima of the Hour
Georgio de Chirico

Again, the painting feels disorienting, much like Jesus' exhortation to love our enemies. The structure around the fountain in the bottom center and the roofline suggests a central point of view, while the arches indicate a viewpoint from the left side of the painting, closer to the perspective of the individual dressed in white.

There are two regions, a region of light in the lower left of the painting and the darker architectural area. The light space is the kingdom of God. The dark architectural area makes up the second region. Those in that realm are in darkness, outside the Kingdom.

A person dressed in white stands in the light. Rocks lay on the ground near him. The red area around his shoulders suggests blood, perhaps due to the throwing of stones. He faces towards the darkness, bows his head, and prays for those in the shadows.

On the first floor of the architectural structure is a man dressed in dark clothing. (He is located inside the second archway from the right.) The man stands in the darkness with his arms crossed. He has perhaps thrown rocks at the man dressed in white, injuring him.

On the structure's second floor, a small individual leans on the wall, overlooking the plaza.

The Christianized painting depicts the stoning of Stephen in Acts 7:54-60. The man in white would represent the martyr, Stephen. The man on the first floor would suggest those who stoned Stephen. The man on the second floor would represent Saul of Tarsus, who stood by and watched. The light coming in from the left of the image is the light from the opened heavens. Stephen prays for those who stoned him and who watch. He prays that they might be cleansed/baptized in the water that crosses from the darkness into the light.

The Great Reversal – Saul to Saint Paul

1 Timothy 1:15-16

Paul writes:

[15] The saying is trustworthy and deserving of full acceptance, that Christ Jesus came into the world to save sinners, of whom I am the foremost. [16] But I received mercy for this reason, that in me, as the foremost, Jesus Christ might display his perfect patience as an example to those who were to believe in him for eternal life.

Paul loved his enemies. His enemies, first-century Christians, didn't change. He did.

Saul of Tarsus was a Pharisee, son of a Pharisee (Acts 23:6). Luke tells us in the book of Acts that Saul was present at the stoning of Stephen. Luke records that Saul ravaged the early church dragging men and women off, committing them to prison. Paul himself tells of his persecution of the church.

"…formerly I was a blasphemer, persecutor, and insolent opponent." 1 Timothy 1:13a

"…I persecuted the church of God violently and tried to destroy it." Galatians 1:13b

Saul received mercy. He became a new man. Hate was replaced with love. The direction of his life reversed, greatly. Saul was a very intense, driven man who experienced a profound change in his attitude and his actions.

Saul began to use his Roman name Paul sometime after his conversion.

Paul went on missionary journeys to found churches. 13 books of the Bible are attributed to him. These books all begin with "Paul."

Beaten with rods, lashed, and nearly stoned to death, the persecutor of Christians became the servant of Christ who himself became the persecuted.

Paul changed. His view of Christ changed. His view of the law changed. His understanding of Gentiles changed from being outside of God's covenant to the unity of Jew and Gentile in Christ Jesus.

As Paul said, "I received mercy."

Again, we note the effect of Christ's love and mercy on human lives. Furthermore, we see how Paul used his intellectual gifts, drive, and resources to help build the Kingdom.

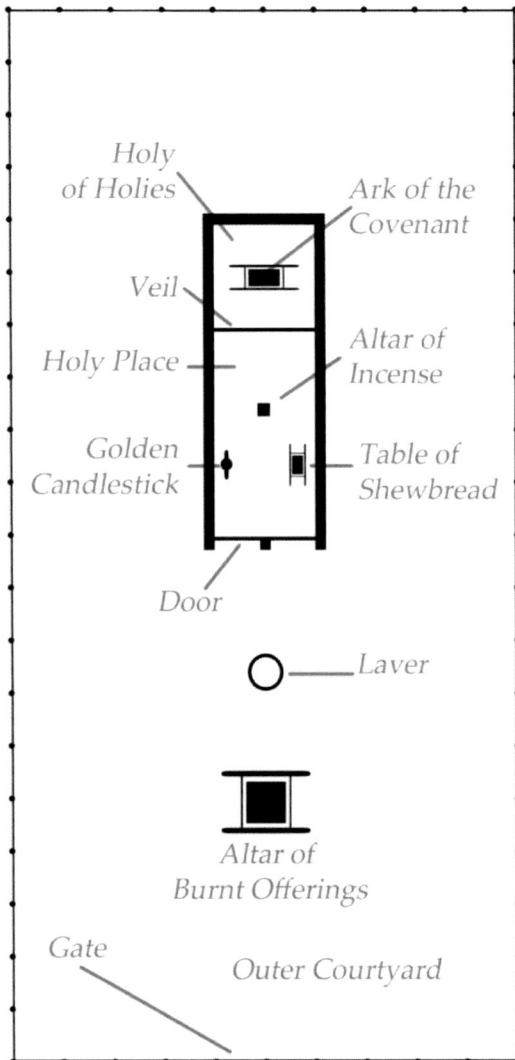

Tabernacle Schematic.

Labels on schematic:
Holy of Holies, *Ark of the Covenant*, *Veil*, *Holy Place*, *Altar of Incense*, *Golden Candlestick*, *Table of Shewbread*, *Door*, *Laver*, *Altar of Burnt Offerings*, *Gate*, *Outer Courtyard*

The Great Christian Reversal – Access to God

A great reversal is enabled within every Christian. If you are a believer in Christ, you have the presence of the Holy Spirit within you. The very presence of God lives inside of you. This spirit will enable you to live, more and more, according to Jesus' great reversal sayings. Over time, you become more Christ-like.

Consider Hebrews 10:19-22

[19] Therefore, brothers, since we have confidence to enter the holy places by the blood of Jesus, [20] by the new and living way that he opened for us through the curtain, that is, through his flesh, [21] and since we have a great priest over the house of God, [22] let us draw near with a true heart in full assurance of faith, with our hearts sprinkled clean from an evil conscience and our bodies washed with pure water.

This passage is referencing the Day of Atonement, also called Yom Kippur.

Context. We go back to the days of Moses beginning with the tabernacle, which is a mobile temple. The tabernacle was divided into two areas. The larger area was the Holy Place. One moved from the outer courtyard into the enclosed Holy Place. The second area was the Holy of Holies, an inner sanctuary where the very presence of God dwelt. The High priest moved from the Holy Place into the presence of God in the Holy of Holies through a curtain on the Day of Atonement.

Under the Covenant with the people of Israel, the High priest entered into the presence of God through the curtain in the tabernacle that separated the Holy Place from the Holy of Holies. Under the New Covenant, the curtain is the flesh of Christ. Jesus, the way, the truth and the life, is the new and living way that enables a believer to enter into "the holy places," into the presence of God.

More context. We also have the nation of Israel, God's chosen people. God's people lived under Levitical law. Exodus 19:5-6

[5] "'Now therefore, if you will indeed obey my voice and keep my covenant, you shall be my treasured possession among all peoples, for all the earth is mine; [6] and you shall be to me a kingdom of priests and a holy nation.' These are the words that you shall speak to the people of Israel."

Sometimes the chosen people broke the law. Breaking the law damaged the relationship between God and his chosen people, so God provided the Priesthood.

The High priest was from the tribe of Levi. The first high priest was Aaron, the older brother of Moses. The role of the High priest was vital. His purpose was to bridge the gap between the people of Israel and God, which came as a result of the law being broken.

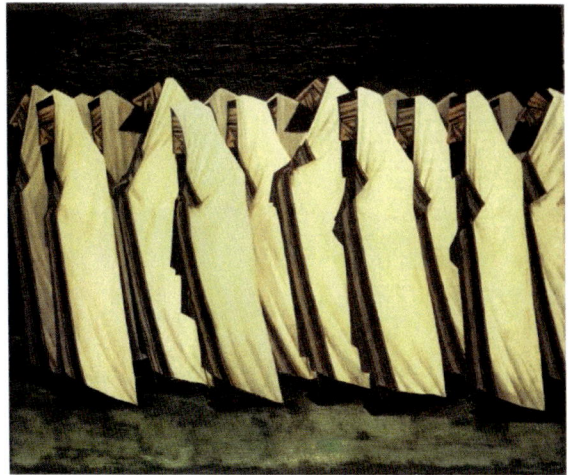

The Day of Atonement
Jacob Kramer

Now we come to the Day of Atonement which occurs once every Hebrew calendar year. The Day of Atonement, or Yom Kippur, is the holiest day of the Hebrew year. For the people of Israel, it is a day when all their past sins would be forgiven. On this day, a comprehensive act of atonement was made for the entire nation.

Preparations for Yom Kippur were made by both the people of Israel and the High priest. The High priest would change out of his high priestly garments into the more ordinary attire of a priest as a sign of humility. A bullock was sacrificed to provide atonement for the high priest and the priesthood. A first goat was sacrificed to provide reparation for the sins of the nation of Israel. Without the shedding of blood, there could be no forgiveness of sins. During the ceremony, the High priest, with the blood collected from the animal sacrifices, entered first into the Holy Place of the tabernacle and then passed through the inner curtain, into the Holies of Holies, into the very presence of God. As part of the ceremony, the sacrificial blood was sprinkled on the Mercy Seat and before the Ark of the Covenant in the

Sacrifice of the Old Covenant
Peter Paul Rubens

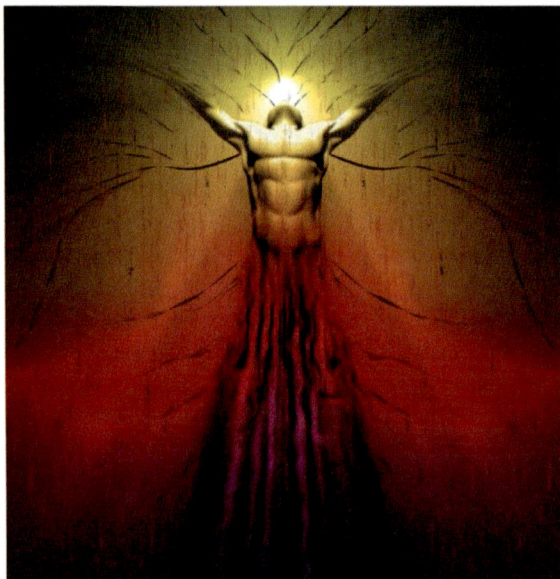

Brow of Grief
Kerry Pierce

Holy of Holies. The blood would also be sprinkled in other locations of the tabernacle, in effect, purifying or cleansing the Tabernacle.

Under the Covenant with the people of Israel, the blood of animals was sprinkled to cleanse the Tabernacle. Under the New Covenant, the blood of Jesus sprinkles our hearts clean. Because we are forgiven, we may enter through the curtain into the presence of God.

Again, this is very good.

Back to the day of Atonement, aka Yom Kippur. Later in the ceremony, outside of the tabernacle, the High priest confesses the nation's sins onto a second goat in front of the people of Israel. This second goat is the scapegoat. The second goat is then taken out into the wilderness, never to be seen again. This portion of the ceremony provided a visual reminder to the people that their sins were removed.

The Scapegoat
William Holman Hunt

William Holman Hunt's painting, *The Scapegoat*, illustrates Leviticus 16:22, "The goat shall bear all their iniquities on itself to a remote area, and he shall let the goat go free in the wilderness." The solitary scapegoat is set against a barren landscape at sunset. Scarlet wool, representing the sins of the nation, is tied to his horns. The goat's feet sink through the salt-encrusted surface of the desert. Bare mountains, dry bones, and dead vegetation create a scene of unrelieved desolation. The goat staggers from thirst, exhaustion, and the unbearable weight of sin. The image recalls the opening line of Psalm 22, "My God, my God, why have you forsaken me?"

Now let's take a look at the work of Christ. The argument made in the *Letter to the Hebrews* is that Jesus is a new High priest. He is a High priest on the order of Melchizedek, a priesthood that is superior to the Levitical priesthood.

Because Jesus was sinless, he did not require a blood sacrifice as the Levitical high priests did. For the sins of the people, all people, he became the blood sacrifice. He also takes on the role of the scapegoat, taking on the sins of the people.

Jesus is then both the superior High priest and the superior blood sacrifice. Jesus' work achieves a superior result. The law is fulfilled, and we enter into a new era of grace.

The author of the Hebrews is saying that Jesus is the new and living way and that he has opened up the curtain to allow us access to the very presence of God. This privilege is made possible for us because we have been sprinkled clean by the sacrificial blood of Christ. Right now.

Christians, in Christ, we are a royal priesthood and a Holy Nation. (See 1 Peter 2:9)

Access to God sounds strange, but the believer has been granted access to God through the blood of Christ. Through Christ, we have a unique level of permissions.

Put another way, Christians are a new Holy of Holies where God's Spirit resides and provides us with continuous access to the Trinity.

Can this be true?

Yes, this is true; you find this described by John and Paul.

1 Cor. 3:16 "Do you not know that you are God's temple and that God's Spirit dwells in you?"

1 Cor. 6:19 "Or do you not know that your body is the temple of the Holy Spirit who is in you, whom you have from God?"

1 John 4:13 "By this we know that we abide in him and he in us, because he has given us of his own Spirit."

Yes, you are packing the Holy Spirit.

Nice, but what does this mean for a believer? It means a great reversal is going on in your life! Right now.

1 Corinthians 2:10-13 (ESV)

[10b] For the Spirit searches everything, even the depths of God. [11] For who knows a person's thoughts except the spirit of that person, which is in him? So also no one comprehends the thoughts of God except the Spirit of God. [12] Now we have received not the spirit of the world, but the Spirit who is from God, that we might understand the things freely given us by God. [13] And we impart this in words not taught by human wisdom but taught by the Spirit, interpreting spiritual truths to those who are spiritual.

Note especially: "not the spirit of the world, but the Spirit who is from God,"

If Captain Barbossa was a Christian, he might say: "That's a lot of long words, Paul. We're naught but humble Christians. What is it you are saying,

Pentecost
Titian

exactly?"

Paul says that by using our minds, asking questions, reading and reflecting on the Bible, listening to sermons, and praying, we enable the Holy Spirit to work within us. We become less like the world and grow spiritually, growing more and more Christ-like over time. We are salt and light in the world and will bear fruit for the Kingdom during our lives.

Psalm 1
Kerry Pierce

Instead you thrill to God's Word,

you chew on Scripture day and night.

You're a tree replanted in Eden,

bearing fresh fruit every month,

Never dropping a leaf,

always in blossom.

Psalm 1:2-3 MSG

To Gain Life, One Must Give it Up

Luke 9:23-26

²³ And he said to all, "If anyone would come after me, let him deny himself and take up his cross daily and follow me. ²⁴ For whoever would save his life will lose it, but whoever loses his life for my sake will save it. ²⁵ For what does it profit a man if he gains the whole world and loses or forfeits himself? ²⁶ For whoever is ashamed of me and of my words, of him will the Son of Man be ashamed when he comes in his glory and the glory of the Father and of the holy angels."

Just before the passage above, Jesus foretells his death.

Luke 9:21-22

²¹ And he strictly charged and commanded them to tell this to no one, ²² saying, "The Son of Man must suffer many things and be rejected by the elders and chief priests and scribes, and be killed, and on the third day be raised."

Later in chapter 9 of Luke, Jesus again foretells of his death to the disciples. Finally, in Luke 18, Jesus tells the disciples of his forthcoming death a third time. Jesus wants his followers to be clear on this particular point, hence the use of repetition in his teaching method.

Jesus must suffer, be rejected by the elite, and then be killed. Following this, he will be resurrected. In Luke 9:23-26, Jesus is laying out what the conditions of service are for a disciple. Disciples are to follow Christ, to imitate Christ. Put another way, to follow in his footsteps.

But dear Jesus, you suffered, you were rejected, and you were killed. By following you as a disciple, does this mean that I might expect some measure of what you went through? Please tell me that this is all figurative and that I

Christ Crucified
Diego Velázquez

don't need to take it literally.

In verse 23, Jesus gives three conditions: Deny yourself, take up your cross, and follow me. Put another way, disciples, lose your life to save it.

Deny yourself, that is, forget about your worldly self-interest and self-fulfillment. What the world offers frequently does not align with what benefits a person spiritually. Think of Jesus turning down Satan's offer of all the kingdoms of the world. Our lives belong to Christ. His will be done.

Take up your cross daily. Cross bearing, in the time of Jesus and now, is a public activity. For Jesus, cross-bearing was quite literal. For disciples today, cross-bearing is generally symbolic. It consists of daily, open submission to the authority of God. The disciple has an option of gaining the world's acceptance or giving their life to Christ daily. Cross bearing is a public confession of Christ. Social media offers an opportunity for daily public acknowledgment of Christ. Peter struggled with this point when he denied Jesus three times. It's not always easy.

Follow me, that is to imitate Christ, to respond to Jesus and his teaching. Again, Jesus' disciples struggled with this in a very literal way after the arrest of Jesus in the garden. They fled. Later, after the resurrection and the indwelling of the Holy Spirit, the disciples moved forward boldly, even to the point of martyrdom.

Jesus challenges us. But, there is great hope. Life in this world is temporary. We are spiritual beings. We have a soul. Our souls are designed for eternity. They are of higher value than anything this world can offer.

Moving forward as disciples of Christ, we have the knowledge of the resurrection, and we have the Holy Spirit as a companion and enabler on our journey in this life.

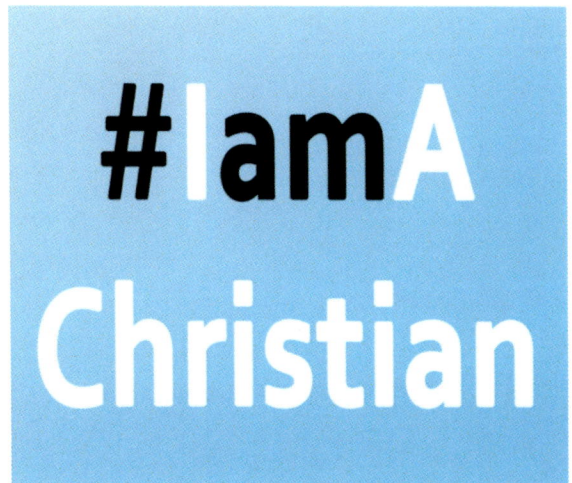

The Man of Dust and the Man of Heaven

1 Corinthians 15:49 Just as we have borne the image of the man of dust, we shall also bear the image of the man of heaven.

To bring this study to a close, I created *The Last Tear*, which depicts three realms: Heaven, transition, and the world.

The Last Tear
Kerry Pierce

The upper realm represents heaven. A young girl has just arrived at an island in heaven. She has entered a spiritual port, where she has been freshly birthed into the afterlife. Everything is still in this realm.

The object that looks like a snowflake is a gathering of angels welcoming her to heaven. The shape of the individual angels echoes that of the girl, but the angels are less defined and smaller than the girl's glorified body.

Again, the egg is a Christian symbol for the resurrection, reminding us of Christ's resurrection from the dead and the promise to believers.

The round element that looks like a moon is the light source of this realm. The glory of

Christ is the light of heaven. A sailboat with sails furled waits on the other side of the island. Christ will escort the girl to the place that he has prepared for her.

The girl of heaven, perfected in body and soul, kneels and looks at the reflections on the glassy sea. Her resurrected body, together with her reflection and her shadow, forms a trinity.

Her shadow represents her forgiven sin. The light of Christ has removed her sin. The shadow falls away from her. The portion of the shadow in the upper realm has already begun to fade. It will disappear entirely, existing only for the briefest moment. The girl of heaven will look at it one last time, smile, and know it is gone forever.

The second realm is the reflections on the surface of the glassy sea. It represents the moments surrounding the end of her earthly life and her transition from the world to heaven. There is motion in this realm. The second sailboat, which brought her to this place, departs under sail after delivering the girl.

The girl's body in heaven bears a resemblance to her reflected earthly body of dust. A believer for many years, empowered by the Holy Spirit, her reflected image resembles the girl of heaven, but ripples distort the reflection as she was not fully perfected while in the second realm.

We are reminded of Christ's physical appearance after his resurrection. "Just as we have borne the image of the man of dust, we shall also bear the image of the man of heaven."

The image contains a third realm, a region underneath the reflecting surface of the glassy sea. This area represents the world, the girl's time on earth, and her journey to Christ during her earthly life. Here we see a dolphin. Dolphins are often used in Christian art as a symbol. George Ferguson's book, *Signs and Symbols in Christian Art*, states, "Generally, it [the dolphin] has come to symbolize resurrection and salvation. Considered to be the strongest and swiftest of the fishes, it was often shown bearing the souls of the dead across the water to the world

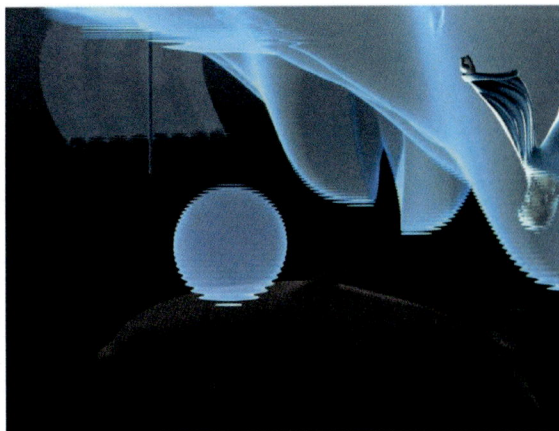

beyond. Depicted with an anchor or a boat, it symbolized the Christian soul, or the Church being guided toward salvation by Christ."[12]

The Last Tear. At the end of her earthly life, the girl of dust is rotated upwards by the host of angels into heaven. As she transitions from earth to heaven, the tear in her eye falls away at the moment of death. This tear is the last tear she will shed.

Text References

1. Pierce, Kerry M. 2017, *Christian Mandalas: The Great Reversal Study.* Gordian Productions.

2. Lane, William L. 2004, *Hebrews: A Call to Commitment*, Page 37. Vancouver, British Columbia: Regent College Publishing.

3. Coffman, James Burton. 1976, *Commentary on Luke.* Houston, Texas: Firm Foundation Publishing House.

4. Bruner, Frederick Dale. 2012, *The Gospel of John: A Commentary*, Page 762. Grand Rapids, Michigan: Wm B. Eerdmans Publishing Co.

5. Stein, Robert H. 1992, Luke, Page 108. Boardman Press.

6. Hawkins, Greg L., and Parkinson, Cally. 2011, *Move: What 1,000 Churches Reveal About Spiritual Growth*, Page 249. Grand Rapids, Michigan: Zondervan.

7. Breton, André. 1924, *Le Manifeste du Surréalisme.*

8. Medina, John J. 2008, *Brain rules, 12 Principles for Surviving and Thriving at Work, Home, and School*, Page 279. Seattle, Washington: Pear Press.

9. Medina, John J. 2008, *Brain rules, 12 Principles for Surviving and Thriving at Work, Home, and School*, Page 279-280. Seattle, Washington: Pear Press.

10. Barclay, William. 2001, *The Gospel of Luke (The New Daily Study Bible)*, Page 269. Louisville, Kentucky: Westminster John Knox Press.

11. Bock, Darrell L. 1994, *Luke 9:51-24:53 (Baker Exegetical Commentary on the New Testament)*, Page 589. Grand Rapids, Michigan: Baker Academic.

12. Ferguson, George Wells. 1959, *Signs and Symbols in Christian Art*, Page 10. New York, New York: Oxford University Press.

Image References

- *Entering Munchkinland, The Wizard of Oz.* Metro-Goldwyn-Mayer. Retrieved from https://peelslowlynsee.wordpress.com/2010/02/25/me-and-the-colorful-world-of-oz/ on May 20, 2018. Low-resolution images were used.
- *The Melancholy of Departure,* Giorgio de Chirico. Public domain US.
- *SLAC National Accelerator Laboratory.* https://www.flickr.com/photos/slaclab/sets/72157647070201514, retrieved March 5, 2018. Used with permission.
- *The Enigma of the Arrival and the Afternoon,* Giorgio de Chirico. Public domain US.
- *Christ and the Good Thief,* Titian. Public Domain.
- *Jesus Washing Peter's Feet,* Ford Madox Brown. Public domain US.
- *The Pharisee and the Publican,* James Tissot. Public domain US.
- *The Great Metaphysician,* Giorgio de Chirico. Public domain US.
- *The Song of Love,* Giorgio de Chirico. Public domain US.
- *The Man Who Hoards,* James Tissot. Public domain US.
- *The Enigma of the Oracle,* Giorgio de Chirico. Public domain US.
- *The Return of the Prodigal Son,* Rembrandt. Public domain.
- *The Prodigal Son in a Tavern,* Rembrandt. Public domain.
- *The Return of the Prodigal Son,* James Tissot. Public domain US.
- *The Prodigal Son,* Giorgio de Chirico. Public domain US.
- *The Return of the Prodigal Son,* James Tissot. Public domain US.
- *Vendredi Saint,* Giorgio de Chirico. Public domain US.
- *The Good Samaritan,* Vincent van Gogh. Public domain US.
- *The Good Samaritan,* Rembrandt. Public domain.
- *The Good Samaritan,* James Tissot. Public domain US.
- *Cheech – 1964 Chevy Impala SS, Up in Smoke.* Paramount Pictures. Retrieved from https://www.leafly.com/news/lifestyle/how-up-in-smoke-changed-history on May 20, 2018. Low-resolution image used.
- *Woman at the Well,* Carl Bloch. Public domain US.
- *Crucifixion, Seen from the Cross,* James Tissot. Public domain US.
- *Jesus Counsels Nicodemus,* William Hole. Public domain US.
- *The Enigma of the Hour,* Giorgio de Chirico. Public domain US.
- *Day of Atonement,* Jacob Kramer. Public domain US.
- *Sacrifice of the Old Covenant,* Peter Paul Rubens. Public domain.
- *The Scapegoat,* William Holman Hunt. Public domain US.
- *Pentecost,* Titian. Public domain.
- *Christ Crucified,* Diego Velázquez. Public domain.

About the Author

Kerry Pierce holds an MS and a BS in Electrical Engineering from Stanford University and a BS in Engineering-Physics from Pacific Lutheran University. Kerry's passions include art, Surrealism, technology, symbolism, math, and Christianity. He has worked in Silicon Valley and Hollywood, authoring books, technical publications, patents, film, and fine art. Kerry has received awards for both his technical work and his art. He has traveled extensively through the Orient and has a great love for synthesizing new ideas from diverse cultures and fields of thought.

Made in the USA
Las Vegas, NV
04 September 2021